FIAT & ABARTH
500
& 600
Colour Family Album

Fiat 500F, 1966

Dedication
This book is dedicated to our very good friends John & Rhian Prosser.

First published in 1998 by Veloce Publishing Plc., 33, Trinity Street, Dorchester DT1 1TT, England. Fax: 01305 268864.

ISBN: 1 874105 80 4/UPC: 36847 00080 6

British Library Cataloguing in Publication Data -
A catalogue record for this book is available from the British Library.

Typesetting (Avant Garde), design and page make-up all by Veloce on AppleMac.
Printed in Hong Kong.

FIAT & ABARTH 500 & 600

& 600

Colour Family Album

VELOCE PUBLISHING PLC
PUBLISHERS OF FINE AUTOMOTIVE BOOKS

THANKS

We would like to thank the following people for their help with this book.

Charlie Hilm, Ingrid Knecht, Henk Ten Cade, Philippe Bacquaert, Ranaud Beckers, Willem & Anna Derksen, Wolfgang Lichtenfels, Yves Doyer, Piero Mossenta, Gerlinde Reichel, Jean-Claude Lefebvre, Marie-Laurence Decke, John Savelkouls, Ronald Cryns and Reinhilde Dehandschutter of Cryns Carrosserie in the town of Mortsel (Belgium), Alois Lenz, Jacques Laubignat, Patrizia Capuzzo, Dick and Martin Elings of the Fiat 500 Club Netherlands, and last, but by no means least, Paul Salmon, Dominique Rival, Clothilde Riviere-Prost, Marie-Hélene Langlois, Véronique Joncheray, Cécile Stragier and Aude Beaupere of Catimini SA.

Abarth 695SS and 595SS, from 1964.

CONTENTS

Abarth-based 500, by Autoparazione of Tiriolo, Italy, is difficult to miss. (Fiat 500 Abarth 1969)

INTRODUCTION

There are a great many cars that would look silly painted bright pink. There are even more that would look plain stupid with their top removed and a fringed fabric oblong in its place. Then again, how would the average car look with no doors and seats like shopping baskets? It takes a car of particular character to emerge from such a transformation looking fabulous - and the Fiat 500 has character out of all proportion to its size.

The Fiat 500 may be described as the true successor to Fiat's much-loved Topolino, and even smaller sibling of the capacious yet diminutive 600.

It has turned up in many forms: estate car, off-roader, beach car, racing car ... and is renowned as practical, cheap everyday transport for many people, in Italy and throughout the world. Small wonder the 'Bambino' still has such a huge following – a small wonder is just what it is.

Ghia 500 Jolly, from 1957.

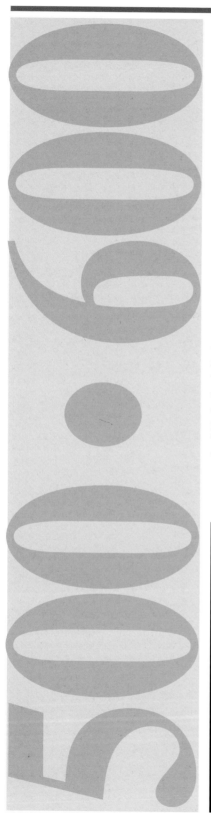

SMALL CAR, BIG STORY

The Fiat story begins in 1899, with the purchase of a motorised tricycle by a dashing young cavalry officer named Giovanni Agnelli. Agnelli was intrigued by the new internal combustion engines and spent much of his spare time tinkering with them. He had a good head for business, too, and could see the huge potential offered by the fledgling motor industry. In Germany and France, in particular, this industry was growing rapidly, and Agnelli was aware that Italy would soon be left behind in the race unless something was done. He believed that he was the man for the job, and soon found two like-minded entrepreneurs, with influence and cash, to work with him. In July 1899, in the city of Turin, *Fabbrica Italiana Automobili Torino* was founded.

Agnelli's prime aim was to

All roads lead to Rome, but how many cars can go from Turin to Rome on less than a tankful?

Being so small, the 500 can go where other cars cannot; only a bicycle competes in Amsterdam. (500R 1973)

With the 500, Fiat were definitely on the right track. (500F 1969)

get a small, light car into production as soon as possible. He was convinced that this would be the best foundation for success, offering the chance of good sales in both the short and the long term. He could push ahead quickly in this direction, too, because he knew of a small car already built in prototype form, but with little or no chance of getting into production. This car had been conceived by Giovanni Ceirano (who manufactured bicycles), and Aristide Faccioli had designed it. Agnelli bought the patents to the car from Ceirano, and employed Faccioli to oversee its development.

The team worked fast. A site was rapidly acquired in Turin, and the new factory began operating early in 1900. Agnelli was able to hold an official opening for the Fiat factory in March, and to present the first examples of the new car. The 3.5hp 'Tipo-A' was a charming little car, capable of just over 20mph. Only eight were built before the need for more speed dictated a larger 6hp engine.

Fiat continued to develop steadily throughout the early 1900s. The larger cars dominated, both in the private sector and on the track. Fiat cars were performing well in road races, and were also taking speed records.

1914 arrived and, with it, the need to concentrate on commercial transport for the

The Italians took the 500 to their hearts — in the country as well as in the town.

war effort. Vehicles were needed in quantity, and quickly, and such demands naturally result in methods of mass-production, however rudimentary. Agnelli was quick to see the advantages of this approach, and considered how to apply mass-production techniques to his cars. Once the war was over, he undertook some research on the production and marketing of a small car of just 500cc. He concluded that the time for such an innovation was not yet right – although he was convinced that its day would come. Throughout the 1920s

and early 1930s, Fiat developed their mid-range and luxury vehicles. Sales were good: the range was wide, and the cars were reliable and well-respected. The only gap in what they had on offer was at that mass-market end, considered by Agnelli some fifteen years earlier.

The answer to the problem was the Topolino, which captivated Italian hearts from the start. It was introduced in 1936, and remained in production throughout the war years and for the following decade. Then, in 1955, it was replaced with the 600 and,

two years later, with the Nuova 500. The much-loved 500 continued, with few changes, until 1975. Three years earlier a new small Fiat, the 126, had been introduced, and the last of the 500s - the 500R - shared the newcomer's floorpan and bigger 594cc engine.

The 126 concept was basically that of an updated 500. One of the major complaints it received was that the popular sunroof had gone; Fiat rectified this un-Italian behaviour in 1974 with the introduction of the 126L. Two years later, the 126 'de Ville'

Practical - and fun to own and drive. (500R 1974)

arrived with a larger 652cc engine. In 1987, there was a big change for the baby Fiat. Although from the outside there was no dramatic difference, the 126 'Bis' was a hatchback, capable of taking a surprising amount of luggage, especially with the rear seat folded flat. It also had a new engine – a water-cooled 704cc unit, positioned on its side under the floor of the luggage space. There were improvements to the interior, too; better seats and more comprehensive instruments. The 126 Bis was produced for Fiat by FSM in Poland.

The latest baby Fiat – the 'Cinquecento' – was first presented to the public in Rome at the end of 1991. Like the 126 Bis, the Cinquecento is built by FSM in Poland. Its design and development process has been quite unlike that of any of the previous baby Fiats. The advent of computer-aided design has helped evolve a 'big on the inside, small on the outside' car, conforming with all the safety and ecological dictates of modern-day motoring (both legal requirements and those essential for successful product marketing). There is a

Two Italian passions (albeit in Belgium) - small cups of strong coffee and small Fiats. (500L 1970)

Rounded lines and perfect proportions contribute to the 500's endearing character. (500F 1968)

Still more Italian passions: pasta, pizza and small Fiats. (500F 1966)

choice of engine: the 704cc, based on the 126 Bis unit, and a 903cc with catalytic converter. The Cinquecento is practical around town and, as one would expect, is a fun car to be associated with. To be worthy of the Fiat 500 name, it also comes complete with plenty of Italianesque style!

The 500's replacement, the 126. Here it is in cabriolet form, as built by FSM in Poland. (126P0P 1993)

The 500 for the 'nineties - the 500 (say cinquecento!). (Cinquecento 1991)

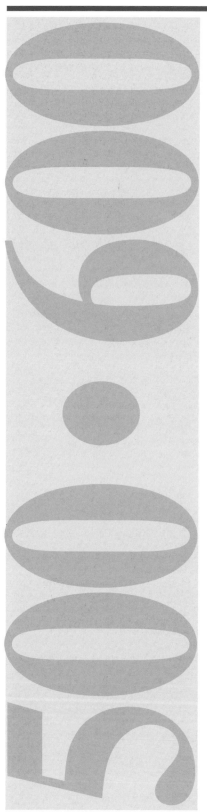

TOPOLINO

Dante Giacosa was born in Rome in 1905. He studied for his engineering degree at Turin Polytechnic, where contact with pioneers of the aviation and motoring industries encouraged his love of all things mechanical, and cars in particular. At the age of twenty-three, Giacosa joined SPA (*Societa Piemontese Automobili*), which became part of the Fiat organisation shortly afterwards.

The young Giacosa began proving his worth immediately. As well as possessing natural talents for both design and engineering, he had the ability to consider a problem from every viewpoint, and more often than not came up with an inspired solution. In 1934 Giacosa – not yet thirty

Below and opposite: Aluminium-bodied Fiat 500 Sport Barchetta, based on a 1937 500 chassis and fitted with 569cc, 20hp engine. It is the only one of its kind.

NSU-Fiat Roadster from 1939, based on a 1938 500 chassis, fitted with 569cc, 20hp engine. The all-steel body is by Weinsberg.

years old – presented his bosses at Fiat with his ideas for the small, affordable car they were looking for. Dr Antonio Fessia, who was in charge of the project, gave him the task of designing the engine and chassis; the bodywork was to be styled by Rodolfo Schaeffer.

The task facing the team was a formidable one. The cars needed to be inexpensive to manufacture, cheap to run, and must be comfortable and practical (able to carry two adults and either two children or 50kg of luggage). The Fiat board had set a price guide of 5000 lire, which must have seemed a depressingly near-impossible budget, and, naturally, any Italian car had to have style.

Giacosa lost no time in searching for solutions. By the

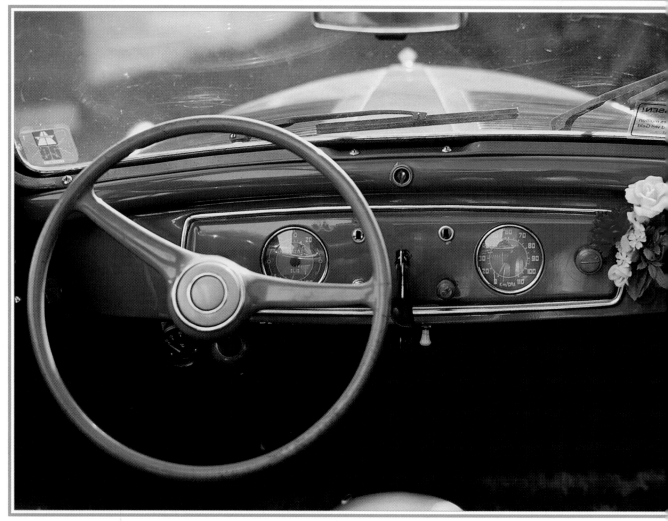

The Topolino lost a little of its classic styling when it was revamped as the 500C. The interior shows its minimum of instrumentation - no more than absolutely necessary. (500C, from 194

summer of 1934, final drawings for the 'Zero A' were on the drawing board. Schaeffer's elegant design for the body provided little space, but Giacosa's solution was to place the 569cc water-cooled engine ahead of the front wheels. The chassis was a simple and practical A-frame design. The first prototype A was tested in October, performing admirably, if a little noisily. A redesigned crankshaft cured the noise problem on the second prototype, which also featured slight bodywork revisions.

The 500, as it was officially known, was launched in June 1936. It was immediately heralded as the world's smallest four-cylinder production car, and was christened 'Topolino'. (This literally means 'little mouse', a name shared in Italian by Mickey, but simply a term of affection when applied to the little Fiat!) The Topolino could be bought for

8900 lire – over-budget, but still reasonable – and it sold well from the start, with production soon reaching one hundred per day. With its simple design, a top speed of 53mph and fuel consumption of 48mpg, the little car was practical, attainable and sustainable. The Topolino A was launched initially as a saloon only, the most popular version having a full-length folding sunroof. A commercial van version was also brought out at the end of that year.

There were some revisions to the Topolino in 1938, including upgrading of the rear suspension but, minor modifications apart, the A remained in production for twelve years, including wartime. Over 11,2000 were built before the 500B made its debut at the Geneva Motor Show in 1948.

With the exception of a few minor cosmetic changes, the 500B looked just the same as its predecessor. However, it differed in having a more powerful engine – still 569cc, but 16.5bhp instead of 13bhp – and so the gearbox and clutch, brakes and suspension were all upgraded to take account of the extra power. The Giardiniera Belvedere estate version of the 500B was launched later that same year. It was capable of carrying four passengers and 50kg of luggage, and was therefore a more practical option for families, although it was slightly slower and less frugal than its saloon counterpart. Its attractive 'woody' styling - in polished ash with masonite panels - gave it a character all its own, although the strong family likeness was still there.

The 500B was to last for just a year, although in that short time 21,000 Bs rolled off the production lines.

The 500C arrived at Geneva in 1949, completely restyled and with all the advantages of extra luggage space. Although less classical and more modern in shape, the 500C lost no fans; in fact, popularity increased. In 1952 the Giardiniera Belvedere estate was joined by the Belvedere all-metal version, its two-tone paintwork echoing the 'woody' panel shape. The ability of these models to carry

The Giardiniera Belvedere in its all-metal version – a practical alternative to the saloon. (from 1954)

four people and luggage assured their continued popularity, and the van version of the Topolino – now in 500C guise - had its devotees, too. The vehicle had a bench seat at the front and a grille to keep occupants and load apart. It was not capacious, but it was ideal for the small business - and was inexpensive enough to make good commercial sense.

Although so very Italian in nature, the Topolino was also built by Simca in France under licence, the first models being known as the Simca 5, and the 500C equivalent the Simca 6. It was also produced under licence in Austria by Steyr-Puch, and in Germany by NSU-Fiat in Heilbron.

Giacosa had become assistant director of Fiat's car division at the beginning of 1940, and he was already working on two possibilities for the Topolino's replacement: a smaller 400 and a larger 700. Neither car was destined to go into production, however: the 700 project was abandoned when Italy entered the war; the 400 project was looking hopeful, but came to an abrupt halt when the entire design facilities, along with the only 400 prototype in existence, were lost in a devastating allied bombing raid. So, as it happened, production of the 500C continued until 1955, during which time more than 37,6000 were produced, making a Topolino tally of over half a million in all.

The Topolino was also built in France as the Simca 5. (Simca 5, from 1936)

Seats for two in style – and a little more room for luggage on the back.
(500C, from 1949)

The Topolino van was ideal for the small business. It was small on the outside, big on the inside. (From 1954)

The first 500 estate car was the Topolino Giardiniera; sometimes seating for two just wasn't enough. (Giardiniera, from 1953)

FIAT 600

Replacing the adored Topolino was not a task to be undertaken lightly. However, the Fiat board had a clear idea of what they wanted - a four-seater saloon capable of at least 85kph (53mph), weighing no more than 450kg (992lb). They also required it to be cheaper to produce than the Topolino had been.

Giacosa realised that the major problem was that of weight. His bosses' suggestion – a front-engined car with rear drive - was a non-starter, especially as a four-seater. He looked briefly at front-wheel drive, but cost ruled that one out straight away.

So Giacosa decided that the engine would need to be astern. Next, he had to change the type of engine. The two-cylinder, air-cooled unit he had hoped for, with three-speed automatic gearbox, was abandoned on grounds of weight and performance, to be replaced with a more conventional four-cylinder, in-line, water-cooled unit with four-speed box. Unlike its predecessor, the new car would be of unitary construction, rather than

Opposite left and this page: The Fiat 600 replaced the Topolino in the garages of Italy and bowed out at the end of the 1960s, when 1.5 million had been built. The 600's 633cc, water-cooled engine was replaced by a 767cc unit with the introduction of the 600D. (600D 1963)

having a separate chassis. The Fiat board approved his ideas, but made their Chief Engineer less happy in his work by asking him to have the finished designs ready within four months. Of course, Giacosa obliged, virtually hibernating with his design team, and by the start of 1953 prototypes were being tested.

There were some nagging problems, particularly with stability. The faults - after much testing and tweaking - were traced to the steering. The performance of the 16hp 570cc engine was considered inadequate, too, so the engine was uprated to 633cc, giving 19hp. The Fiat board was satisfied, and the go-ahead was given. While production facilities were being tooled up in readiness, further cars were built for testing and training purposes. Fiat mechanics would not be expected to attack a customer's pride and joy unprepared.

Although compact, the 600's interior made use of every last millimetre of available space.

A Fiat with a fringe on top: Ghia produced a Jolly based on the Multipla, too. (Ghia 600 Jolly, 1956)

The 600 was also built in Germany by Neckar (NSU-Fiat), and was badged as the Jagst. (Jagst 770)

(Surprisingly, not every manufacturer has introduced each new model with this degree of forethought!)

Early in 1955 the new Fiat 600 was unveiled to the press in the wintry and mountainous regions of northern Italy. Fiat were so confident of their new protégé that they were happy to put it through its paces in the most arduous of conditions; if it could prove itself there, surely it would make a good impression anywhere? It did not let them down – words such as 'outstanding', 'miraculous' and 'unbelievable' were heard from journalists as often as their remarks about

The ingeniously designed 600 Multipla - the 600 stretched - with the load-carrying space in the centre. It was the first real MPV. (600 Multipla, 1962)

the cold or their need for a drink!

In the more hospitable surroundings of the Turin Motor Show that April, the Fiat 600 was introduced to the public. Many of the independent coachbuilders offered their own rhapsodies on a 600 theme, something that was to become a regular feature of Fiat model launches. At just over 3.2 metres in length, and with seating for four with limited space for luggage behind the rear seat, the 600 was an ideal family car. Priced at 59,0000 lire – under £300 – it was within reach of the Italian in the strada, too, and could turn in a respectable 42mpg.

The 600 could easily be turned into an effective load carrier by flattening the rear seats, whereupon the wide doors gave access to an amazing usable area of luggage space. Aside from unitary construction, one of the major space-savers was the novel layout of the engine and transmission. The cooling system sat alongside the engine, and all the routine servicing points were easily accessible without any double-jointed contortions. Would-be 600 purchasers soon discovered that what the motoring press had reported was true: the 600 was easy to drive and to park, and - thanks to its independent suspension - very stable, even in adverse

The Michelotti-designed Shellette, named after the designer (brother to the driver Harry Schell), first appeared at the Concours d'Elegance d'Allasio in 1967. With basket seats and sunshade, the Shellette is reminiscent of the Jolly. It's also a little like the British Meadows Frisky Microcar, also styled by Michelotti. (Michelotti Shellette 1967)

weather conditions. The interior appointment was simple and practical, with seats that were firm but comfortable, and the heating system was effective.

Sales of the 600 went well. There were no major problems with the car, and owners were generally pleased with their purchase, finding it surprisingly spacious, frugal, reliable and fun. A number of minor changes were effected in 1957: wind-up windows replaced the previous sliders,

dashboard and seats were improved, and the suspension and electrical systems were upgraded. The following year a new, cooler tone was introduced for the interior finish, with a choice of trim colours offered for the first time, and an improved clutch. In 1959, the indicators migrated from the top of the wings to the sides, while the sidelights were repositioned below the headlamps. Despite the uncertain economic situation in Europe in the late 1950s, the 600 kept selling; by 1960, when the 600D superseded it, over

89,0000 examples of the 600 had rolled off the production line.

The major improvement introduced with the 600D was a new engine – 767cc giving 32hp - enabling the car to reach a top speed of 68mph.

The Jagst Riviera convertible – on appearance alone, who would guess its close relationship to the Fiat 600? Jagst Rivieras were made by Neckar and had body styling by Vignale.

The cooling system was improved to match, and the engine cover received extra louvres for better heat dissipation. The louvres, along with the quarter lights now fitted in the front window aperture, and the addition of bumper overriders, were the major external differences between the first 600Ds and the last of the 600s. In 1964 the 'suicide' doors were replaced with front-hinged ones, and the following year the 600D gained new light clusters but lost its side trim, while the front was restyled, incorporating the squarer Fiat badge. The 600D continued in production in this form until 1969, by which time more than 1.5 million had been made. By now, of course, sales of the 500 had

Ghia's Jolly version of the 600 (see chapter 5) earned its stripes on the beach, the golf course ... wherever posing was possible. (Ghia 600 Jolly 1956)

sembled for the Austrian market by Steyr-Puch, by Zastava (then in Yugoslavia), in Argentina, and by SEAT in Spain, which served all the export markets from 1970.

When the decision was taken to go for a rear-engined replacement for the Topolino, Giacosa realised that the solving of one problem had created another, rather serious one. Demand for the Belvedere estate version of the Topolino was still high, and rising, but it would be impossible to create an estate version of the 600 because of the siting of the engine. He knew he was going to have to come up with a solution to preserve Fiat's share of that particular market. Although the problem preoccupied him for a long while, Giacosa's solution was amazingly simple. He decided to stretch the 600, creating the load space in the middle, rather than at either end. The front seating was moved as far forward as possible, right over the front wheels, which dictated a universally jointed steering column and upgraded suspension. Three rows of seats provided accommodation for six, with the back (or back and middle) rows flattening completely for an astounding amount of load space. As an

long passed the 1.5 million mark, and Fiat's 'larger smaller car' torch had been taken up by the 850, introduced in 1964, of which 2.3 million would be sold over its seven-year production life.

The 600 was also built in Germany from 1960 by Neckar (formerly called NSU-Fiat), and was badged as the Jagst 770. Coupé and convertible versions of the Jagst, known as the Rivera, were made, too, with coachwork designed by Vignale. 600s were also as-

Inspired by boat design. Fiat's own styling department produced two examples of this wonderful car, based on the 600, for the Agnelli family's own use.

The rear seating is more nautical than automotive ...

alternative, it was possible to order two bench seats, front and middle, giving permanent luggage space at the rear. Access was via two wide doors, hinged to the same pillar.

After some initial reluctance on the part of Fiat management to risk such an unconventional arrangement, the appropriately named Fiat 'Multipla' went into production in 1956. It was warmly received, the most common first reaction being one of disbelief that a car so tiny really could deliver the goods. On first introduction, the Multipla was fitted with a 633cc, 21.5hp engine. As with the saloon, the 600D version took over in 1960, fitted with the 767cc, 32hp unit, which increased top speed from 55 to 65mph. Multipla production ceased in 1966; over a decade, more than 16,0000 had been sold.

... so is the detail of the wooden bumpers.

The Siata Spring, based on the 600's replacement, the 850. Siata had produced modified Topolino engines, and later built some modifications on the 500. (Siata Spring circa 1965)

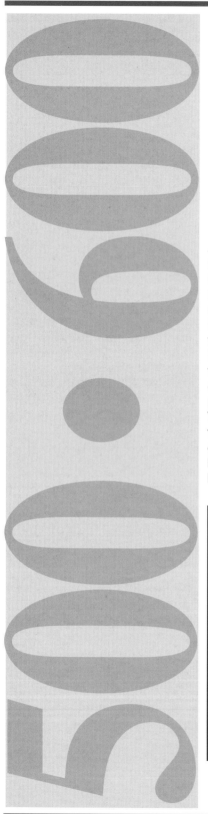

FIAT 500

4

Just after World War 1 Giovanni Agnelli had first considered the concept of a minimalist, mass-produced car; Dante Giacosa had brought that dream to fruition with the Topolino in the 1930s. His 400 project, had it survived, would have updated the concept, but that had disappeared without trace during World War 2. Perhaps there were advantages in having to go back to the drawing board, although that cannot have seemed a convincing argument at the time.

Postwar trends were, of necessity, towards cheap motoring. Scooters had hit the big-time, especially in Italy, but whatever the brochures might have wished you to believe – circus families excepted - two adults, two children under five and a dog cannot make sense of a scooter. Microcars were becoming increasingly popular, too, particularly in Germany - where the Topolino had also carved itself an

The new Italian baby car was introduced to its public in a procession through the Turin streets.

One of the subtle differences between the 500L and earlier 500s – exterior polished metalwork. (500L, from 1968)

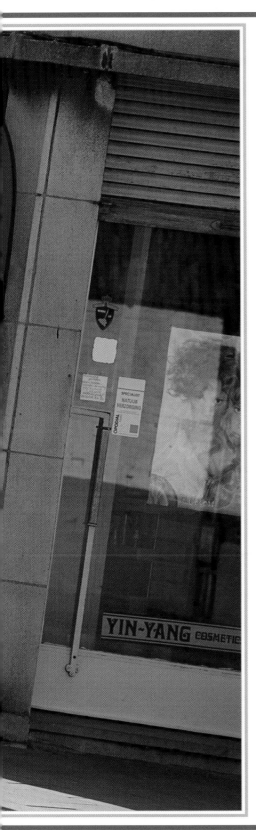

The 500's 'short sunroof' was nonetheless large in proportion to the car and offered a taste of wind in the hair motoring on sunny days. (500F, from 1965)

The badging proclaimed 'Nuova 500' right up until introduction of the 500L in 1968. For the first eight years of its life, the 500 was fitted with rear-hinged 'suicide-doors.' (500D 1960)

excellent market. Giacosa also had the primary design work of the 600 to draw on – and, after that car's launch in 1955, vindication of the ideas behind it. His idea for the new car was that it should be complementary to the 600, not its replacement. His new project became known as the '400' (old habits die hard), and the new had a great deal in common with the old, both conceptually and practically.

Giacosa's aim was to keep things as simple as possible.

An air-cooled engine at the rear would power the car, primarily a two-seater with capacity to take children or luggage at the back; its brief was to provide basic motoring for all. Weight was to be kept down to 370kg, fuel consumption up to 60mpg, and sufficient performance was required for a top speed of 53mph.

Towards the end of 1954 Giacosa was working on the details, with the aim of producing prototypes for testing

by the middle of the following year. But the engine choice brought difficulties, with each member of the management team convinced that his own particular solution to the problems – particularly of vibration, noise and weight – was the only true course to follow. Ultimately, Giacosa's knowledge and reputation won through, and practical, rather than emotional, solutions to the problems were found. All these machinations had wasted a deal of time, however, and only at the beginning of 1956 was the final go-ahead given to start production the following year. Prototypes were built and tested extensively. Giacosa and his team kept going despite a plethora of minor hitches and some major difficulties, and in the face of tragedy, when one of their number was killed during testing.

In July 1957, the motoring press headed for Turin for the press launch of the '500 Nuova'. It was not quite two years since the 600 launch, and so much warmer, giving the more relaxed journalists an ideal opportunity to see Fiat's true replacement for the Topolino at first hand. Comparisons were inevitable, but to the detriment of neither car; the Nuova 500 was well received. It was launched to the public not conventionally at a show, but via a procession through the streets of

A Fiat 500 fits in the smallest of parking places. (500F, from 1965)

46

and improved. The original version was kept as the 'Economy' (although the initial 13hp engine was considered too underpowered even for this face-saving version) and a 15hp unit, still of 479cc capacity, was fitted in both cars. Thus the new Fiat felt less sluggish to drive and increased its top speed from 53 to 56mph. Some modifications were made to cross the important marketing divide between chic basic and plain crude – windows that opened and upholstery on the rear seat being prime examples - although interior and exterior trim and dashboard switchgear were also revamped.

The plan worked. Disaster had been averted; at last, the Topolino had a replacement worthy of the 500 name. Within a year a further model was added – the 500 'Sport'. It was fitted with a 499.5cc engine, which delivered 21.5hp and gave a maximum speed of a terrifying 68mph. There was no sunroof, to provide extra strength. The colour scheme for the Sport was distinctive: grey with a broad red side stripe. It soon lived up to its name, too, notching up class wins at Hockenheim, and rally wins within its first year. During 1959, a short sunroof was made available as an option on the Sport. Sunroofs were the key to dispersing the last of the

Turin, and the little 500 won hearts from the first.

Unfortunately, the euphoria did not convert into instant sales. Despite all the agonising, there was still a major vibration problem, and many potential owners were not impressed by the performance. A rethink was required, so that a nicer finished product – one more suited to the excellent concept that had inspired it - might be launched properly at the Turin show in the autumn.

New 500: take two. The Nuova 500 made its debut at the show as the 'Normale', with a price tag five per cent higher than the original. It had been substantially modified

Perhaps there just wasn't enough seating in a 500 ... (500L 1970)

embarrassment of the fudged launch. The 'Normale' sported its short sunroof, while the 'Economy' became the more exotic 'Transformabile' with full-length roll-back roof.

The new 500 had experienced a troubled first three years, and could so easily have disappeared before it had a chance to prove itself. However, the little car was so bursting with character that its public image survived - supported by the determination and persistence of its creator, Giacosa.

1960 was an important year for the 500. The 500D was introduced, at the same time as the 'D' versions of the 600 and Multipla. The major change was adoption of the 499.5cc, 17.5hp engine, which gave the 500 more energy to compete with cars of larger dimension. As a result, up

went the top speed to 60mph-plus, and up went fuel consumption, to a still respectable 46mpg. The Transformabile was withdrawn, the 500D now available only in the short-sunroof version, and the Sport was discontinued altogether. A folding rear seat-back graced the interior of the 500D, increasing its load-carrying capacity, the fuel tank was reshaped to give slightly more room up front and, on the outside, the rear lights were enlarged. There were few changes ahead for the 500D, other than the fitting of an automatic interior light and windscreen washer, and slight changes to the instrument panel. Some 60,0000 examples were to roll off the production line before the 500D was replaced in 1965.

The next 500 in line was the 500F. It was powered by the

... but help was at hand with the Giardiniera, introduced in 1960. (Giardiniera, from 1960)

The functional interior of the 500F. It was left to the 500L to provide luxuries such as padded fascia and door pockets. (500F, from 1965)

same engine as the 500D, but upgraded to 18hp. The major change to the external appearance was the introduction of front-hinged doors, with the result that the door pillars could be thinner and the windscreen deeper. These modifications combined to give a much more modern appeal, without changing the basic looks or character of the car. On the mechanical side, a modified driveshaft and improved clutch were fitted, and the heating system was enhanced.

In 1968 the 500F was joined

by the 500L (L for Lusso). The outward signs of a new model were subtle, on the whole. Out went the 'Nuova' badging, to be replaced with a discreet 'Fiat 500L'; the front badge was smaller, too. Nudge bars were added, front and rear, and chrome-coloured trim adorned the window surrounds and gutters. The 500L had radials fitted as standard, and smart hubcaps. The instruments inside were considerably updated, to include a fuel gauge (a first for a 500), a redesigned steering wheel and speedometer (courtesy of the 850). Imitation leather was available for the seats (which now reclined), the fascia was padded, carpets replaced rubber mats, and map pockets nested in the doors. Unfortunately, all this luxury meant a ten per cent increase in the

The 500's compact engine, seen here in the more spacious surroundings of the Fiat Weinsberg. (Weinsberg Coupe 1959)

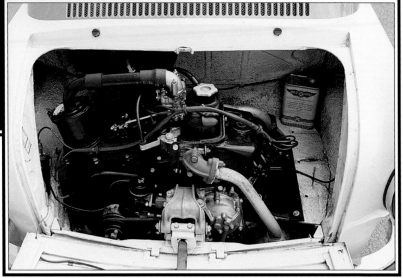

price of the 500L compared to the 500F. These two models made a significant impact, selling almost 2.3 million units before they were withdrawn in 1972.

The final manifestation of the 500 was the 500R. This had a lot in common with the new arrival, the 126. The cars shared a floorpan, and also an engine – now enlarged to 594cc and producing 23hp. The 500R's interior was basically similar to that of the 500F, although some of the 500L options could be specified, at extra cost, when ordering. The front badge had changed to the modern Fiat horizontal strip. Although the 500 was still held in great affection, the 126 was gaining ground in the market, and the 500R did not sell in great numbers. Just 33,4000 rolled off the line before production ended in 1975; total sales of the 500 had reached 3.4million.

Strangely, the 500R was outlasted by one improbable contender. An estate version of the Nuova 500 was introduced early in 1960 and named (shades of Topolino), the 'Giardiniera'. Faced with problems similar to those encountered with the Topolino Giardiniera and the 600 Multipla, Giacosa came up with an inspired solution. He took the 499.5cc engine, turned it on its side and placed it under the rear floor area. It was easily reached through a panel in the floor for maintenance. Access to the large, flat-loading luggage space was through a single left-hinged rear door. Occupants of the back of the car benefited from sliding rear

Autobianchi produced cars with a higher level of specification, based on the 500. (Autobianchi Bianchina, from 1957)

Autobianchi made their version of the Giardiniera, the Panoramica. They also built Fiat's version until 1977. (Autobianchi Panoramica 1968)

windows and a long sunroof.

The extra weight meant that the Giardiniera was not exactly the quickest vehicle around, reaching, perhaps, 55mph with a fair wind behind, but it was certainly a practical one, and it found favour with small businesses and growing families, like its Topolino namesake. Over 16,1000 were sold in the first half of the 1960s. Then there was a three-year break, until 1968, when production of the Giardiniera passed to Autobianchi, who were already making their own version, the 'Panoramica', as well as a commercial van version under the 'Bianchina' name. The Giardiniera continued in production in this form until 1977 - keeping its rear-hinged doors to the end.

Autobianchi had been formed in 1955 with Fiat, Pirelli, and Giuseppe Bianchi. Bianchi's father, Edoardo, had built up a thriving car manufacturing business, but his factory had been destroyed, and the business ruined, during World War 2. Autobianchi became part of the Fiat empire, producing more luxurious versions of their cars (which sold alongside the Fiat-badged ones) and, in 1968, it was taken over completely by the parent company. The first car produced under the Autobianchi name arrived in 1957: the 500-based 'Bianchina', with full-length, roll-back roof. Over 35,000 were sold. A charming Cabriolet version, of which only 9000 were made, followed three years later. In 1962, Autobianchi produced a four-seater Bianchina, which

featured a longer, squared-off cabin to make room for the extra heads. These 'Quattro Posti' survived seven years of production; along the way 69,000 were made.

The charming Bianchina Cabriolet, christened 'Eden-Roc' in France, after the hotel in Antibes where it made its debut. (Autobianchi Bianchina Cabriolet, from 1960)

Growing families liked the Giardiniera's extra space. (The engine was shoe-horned into a gap under the floor, reached by lifting the hatch. (Giardiniera, from 1960)

The Autobianchi four-seater, known in France as the Lutece, may have lost points in its roof styling but the design did give extra headroom. In 1968 Autobianchi was swallowed up by the huge Fiat empire.(Autobianchi 4-posti, from 1962)

FIATS IN DISGUISE

A car of such endearing proportions challenged the major coachbuilders to create for it some imaginative clothing. As part of the Fiat concern, Autobianchi had produced higher-specification versions from the outset, and Abarth had set the 500 on the road to racing success. In Germany, Nekar (formerly NSU-Fiat) brought out their 'Weinsberg' Limousette and Coupé in 1959. Only 6200 emerged over the four years of its production life, although the company also made a small van based on the Giardiniera.

The story of the Austrian company began in 1918. During the 1930s, after Steyr had formed a partnership with the Puch cycle company, it absorbed the ailing Austo-Daimler concern and started

The elegant Moretti Coupe really is a 500. These cars are now extremely rare and precious. (Moretti Coupe, circa 1968)

59

assembling Fiats under licence from Turin. The first Steyr-Puch 500 appeared in 1957, powered by the company's own 493cc engine. Versions with larger engines followed: a powerful 643cc was developed at the end of the 1950s, primarily for use by the Austrian police, and, in 1964, the incredible 650TR was introduced with its powerful 34hp, 650cc engine. In tandem with the saloons, Steyr-Puch also produced the 'Combis' – a sturdy and powerful version of the Giardiniera.

As the immediate postwar years gave way to times of less austerity, so the market for less serious cars began to grow. The coachbuilder, Ghia, responded to the mood with the 'Jolly', a pretty little car with no top, no doors, wicker seats and a removable, fringed fabric hood. The first Jollys were based on the 600, but the best known, based on the 500, was introduced in 1957. The Jolly was exquisitely made, with great attention to detail, and came in bright candy colours. It was an immediate hit – a beach car that looked good anywhere. With its reliance on fine weather, however, it was always going to be a Mediterranean special – no candidate for the north-European export market, this! It became

Perhaps better known for more conservative designs, Ghia nevertheless produced over 700 Jollys, based on the 500, 600, Giardiniera and Multipla. (Ghia 500 Jolly, from 1957)

a favourite with the seriously monied yachting fraternity, and came with rope-eyes to help it from ship to shore. A version of the Jolly was based on the 600 Multipla, and a 500 Giardiniera Jolly was also manufactured from 1964, the only real difference between these and the standard version being the little open-air luggage compartment at the rear for carrying baggage. The Jolly remained in production until 1966, with only around 700 manufactured altogether.

By the age of seventeen, Alfredo Vignale was already well aware of the possibilities of coachbuilding: he was

The Albarella was made in 1967 by the Savio company. They also transformed the 600 into a Jeep lookalike, the Jungla, and, with the stylist Boano, made a 500 convertible beach car. (Savio Albarella 1967)

working as a technician for Pinin Farina. Soon after the end of World War 2, Vignale traded in his old motorbike for a Topolino. The bodywork of this car was very rusty and neglected, so he decided to make it a new aluminium one. This went so well that another Topolino was reclothed, with a view to going into production.

In 1948, Vignale started his own coachbuilding company, which grew rapidly and earned an excellent reputation for first-class workmanship. He designed and built cars for most of the major Italian manufacturers, and also started manufacturing cars under his own name, mostly based upon Fiat models. His first 500-based car appeared in 1958 and was called 'Minnie' – Mouse, not Minor!

The 'Gamine' (French for kid or urchin), based on the 500F, was introduced in 1967 and remained in production until 1970. Just three metres long, it is one of the tiniest of Vignale's cars, offered in a range of interesting colour schemes: blue with yellow interior, yellow with aquamarine, or coral with black. The Gamine - equipped with rope-fixing points for hauling ashore - was also popular with the Mediterranean yachting set. A winter hardtop was available, too. At the end of 1969 Vignale sold his business to DeTomaso. He was killed in a car accident just three days later, at the age of 56.

The Giannini company was founded in Rome by the two brothers, Attillio and Domenico, in 1920. Their first

connections with Fiats involved tuning Topolino engines during the mid-1930s. After the war, the company concentrated on producing sporting prototypes for competition, a field in which they were most successful. When the Fiat 600 was introduced, the company worked on derivations with 750cc and 850cc engines. The arrival of the 500 started off a whole range of Giannini-produced cars based on the little Fiat with the standard 500 engine, as well as some for 600cc and 650cc units. In 1964, a curious reversal of this trend brought an economy Giannini, with a 390cc engine, and three years later an electrically-powered 500 was also marketed.

The Fervès company from Turin transformed the 500 into

a highly practical and rugged little off-roader called the 'Ranger'. Although it had the appearance of a fun car, the Ranger was popular with fire, forestry, electricity and water departments, especially in southern Italy. Mechanically, the Ranger was pure 500, with only minor modifications, although the drive assembly came courtesy of the 600 Multipla. The Ranger had the big advantage of small stature – it could reach places that defeated wider vehicles. The four-seater Ranger was introduced in 1967, with a two-seater pick-up version, called 'Cargo', also available. The following year the 4 x 4 Ranger made its appearance, again based on the 500, but with specially manufactured five-speed gearbox and front drive assembly.

Moretti was another long-established firm of Turin-based coachbuilders to produce an unusual variation on the 500 theme. In 1958, they intro-

The four-seater version of the Ferves Ranger - an unusual 500. (Ferves Ranger 2wd, from 1967)

The Vignale Gamine, another wonderful costume for the 500, and one which has become a classic. The front grille is purely cosmetic. (Vignale Gamine, from 1967)

duced their first, the 'Station Wagon', then - three years later - a 500 Cabriolet and the first version of their elegant Coupé. Gently rounded at the front, squared-off sportingly at the rear, and beautifully finished, the earliest Moretti Coupés are very rare. The car was updated in 1968 with a more angular front, and a sporty 595 SS version was also issued. Only a few hundred or so Moretti Coupés were manufactured, so they are a 500 manifestation of great rarity. During the 1970s, Moretti continued the Fiat theme with some novel examples based on the 126.

We have looked at the renowned coachbuilders and tuners. There were other companies and individuals who found the little Fiat an ideal starting point for some unusual, interesting or brilliant conversions. Lombardi, Brutsch, Frua, Savio, Siata, Viotti, and many others, all produced their own cars, each with distinctive character and that certain 500 finesse.

Steyr-Puch produced their own 500s, with small and large engines. Their 34hp 650cc would certainly leave the 493cc in a cloud of dust. (Steyr Puch 1957)

The Weinsberg was Neckar's (NSU-Fiat) version of the
500. This is a Weinsberg Coupe. A saloon version was
called the Limousette. (Weinsberg Coupe 1959)

The Fiat 500 Barchetta, from designer Peter Stevens, of Lotus, Jaguar and McLaren fame. It has a 30hp, 650cc engine based on that of the 126. (Barchetta 1982)

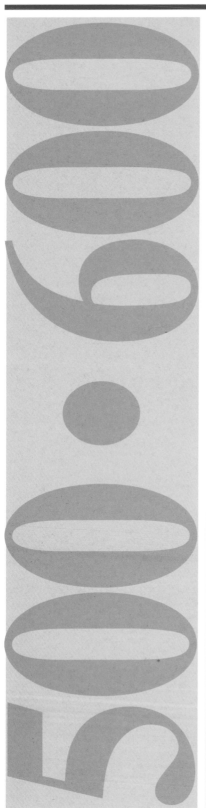

FIAT ABARTH

Karl Abarth was born in Vienna in 1908, on 15 November. The date is significant because his zodiac sign, Scorpio, suggested the emblem for his company.

Young Karl was fascinated by all things mechanical, and found himself a job at the factory of motorcycle manufacturer, MT. He developed a taste for racing when, at short notice, he was asked to ride in the Austrian motorcycle grand prix. He was living with his mother (who was divorced from his father) and, with her agreement, quit his job, using his small inheritance to buy a second-hand motorcycle to launch what he hoped would be a successful racing career.

The 595 SS in road—going guise, introduced in 1964, with the famous scorpion painted on the bonnet. (Abarth 595 SS, from 1964)

This Fiat Abarth 595 SS Assetto Corsa brings joy to the sole. (from 1966)

The engine of the 695 SS. Struts were used to keep the engine cover open for better cooling. (Abarth 695 SS, from 1964)

The 1965 Abarth 1000TC of Leo and Margit Aumuller, in action at the Nurburgring.

Main picture: Not quite the car for a shopping trip – the 695 SS wearing Belgian racing colours. (Abarth 695 SS, from 1964)

More Nurburgring action – the 1962 Fiat Abarth Berlina of Graziano Tessaro and Roberto Chiavacci leads the 1965 1000TC of Reinhold Koster, by a claw.

Karl was taken on by DKW, for whom he had a good deal of success during two years of racing. He also bought a Sunbeam sidecar, and challenged a number of records - the most bizarre of which was a 'point to point' against the Orient Express, which Karl won by almost half an hour at the second attempt! Just before the start of World War 2, Karl was involved in a serious motorcycling accident which ended his racing career. He found a job running a small company in wartime, but it was less than successful and, in 1945 - penniless - he went to visit his father in Italy, reinventing himself in Italian form as 'Carlo' Abarth.

Abarth now met some influential people: Ferry Porsche, the racing driver Nuvolari and Piero Dusio, a rich industrialist from Turin, who were in the process of planning and building the 'Cisitalia' racing car. The thinking was that Cisitalia cars would utilise many Fiat parts, and Dante Giacosa was one of those involved in this part of the process. In the event, things did not go according to plan. The Cisitalia never raced; the company folded; Dusio went to South America.

Porsche set about his 356 project, based on VW rather than Fiat parts, although Abarth would later lend his name to twenty beautiful aluminium-bodied Porsche 356 'Abarth-Carreras', which achieved notable success in the early 1960s. Abarth concentrated on manufacturing specialist tuning systems for racing cars, converting engines for the Turin-based manufacturers.

The Fiat 600, introduced in 1955, was a prime candidate for Abarth's talents. The Fiat Abarth 750 appeared the following year. It was fitted with a modified 767cc engine which could top 80mph and achieve 60mph in less than half the time of the standard car. Three series of 750s for Zagato followed, each performing well in their racing class. In 1956, speed records were achieved with the fabulous aerodynamic bodies built by Bertone and based on Abarth's 600. Maximum speeds of over 120mph were recorded; the following year, top speed was 136mph (clothed in Pininfarina bodywork).

The early 1960s brought the Abarth TC850, based on the 600D, including the specially-prepared Corsa built for racing at the Nürburgring. In 1961, the first version of Abarth's road-going 1000TC was introduced. The 68hp 982cc engine was prepared from the 747cc unit, the car's top speed being 94mph. The second series was introduced three years later, with power increased to 76hp and a top speed of 118mph. Extra cooling was now needed, courtesy of a large radiator at the front end.

Another year ... and yet

The Abarth 595 SS Assetto Corsa – a veritable little powerhouse. (From 1966)

600s, remember.

As soon as the Nuova 500 appeared, Abarth was doing things with it. His version was much gutsier than the original, and immediate orders were taken. Early in 1958, during a week-long endurance event at Monza, a Fiat Abarth 500 completed 11,000 miles at an average speed of 67.5mph. The event was a marketing coup for Fiat, cementing the association with Abarth. Now it was the turn of the 500 to enter the endurance scene, which it did with gusto: Abarth 500s (Pininfarina-bodied) recorded speeds well in excess of 100mph.

The famous Abarth 595 was introduced in 1963. It was based on the 500D, with a modified 27hp, 594cc engine, and a top speed of 75mph-plus. The following year the 595 SS arrived, with a 32hp engine, capable of 78mph. The second series of both 595 and 595 SS models, based on the newly-launched 500F, took over in 1965, continuing in production until 1969. The 595 SS 'Assetto Corsa', produced between 1966 and 1971, was recognisable instantly by its hugely enlarged front bumper section and front-mounted oil cooler.

In 1964, a new Abarth version of the 500D, the Fiat Abarth 695, was introduced to compete in the 700cc racing class. With an engine capacity of 689.5cc and power of 30hp, it could manage a top speed of 80mph. The 695 SS version, introduced in the same year, had 38hp at its disposal to reach 85mph. The second series came along in 1965 (as with the 595). It was

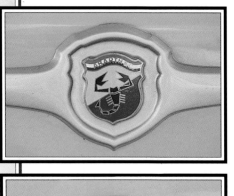

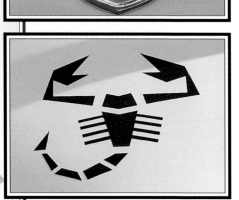

The Abarth Scorpion as portrayed on badges at different times.

more horses. The third series managed 120mph from 80hp engines, and needed extra oil cooling as well. These cars sported disproportionate glassfibre bumpers at the front. Series four: 85hp, 122mph ... and still rising! Yet to come was the 'Radiale' of 1966 (106hp, 130mph), and the 1970 version (112hp, 135mph): all basically Fiat

Above and facing page: A superb rebuild of Abarth's 600-based 850TC – one of Abarth's many succesful racers.

based on the 500F and remained in production until 1971. The 695 SS Corsa was produced between 1966 and 1971 – with a less aggressively styled face than its 595 stablemate. A 695 SS 'Radiale' appeared in 1968, designed specifically to counter opposition in the 700cc racing class.

The Abarth company enjoyed an excellent relationship with Fiat for in excess of twenty years. In 1971, they were bought out by Fiat, becoming part of their massive empire.

GALLERY

Ferves Ranger 2wd from 1967

Ghia Jolly, from 1957

Simca 5, from 1936

Fiat 500R, 1973.

High drama for a little Fiat.

Photographer's Postscript

Those readers familiar with the 'Family Album' series will know of my preferred choice of cameras and lenses. With one exception, this tenth book in the series is no different. I am still working with Leicas and their wonderful lenses, but a hernia operation, accompanied by the doctor's strict instructions on how much weight I should carry, forced me to reduce my arsenal of lenses from eight to three. This I achieved by plugging the critical area of 28mm to 180mm with two Leica zoom lenses - a choice that concerned me, in case image quality should suffer. I need not have worried. The majority of photographs in this book were made with the zooms, including every gallery picture. Film used throughout was Fujichrome Velvia.

I am always surprised by the unlikely regions that take to particular cars. When working on the first two Family Album books, on the Citroen 2CV and DS, I was surprised at how few were collected in France, and how many were to be found in the Netherlands. So with Fiat 500; yes, they are there on the roads in Italy, but so many collectors are in Germany, Holland, Belgium and France. My thanks to the Topolino Club Deutschland, especially to Piero Mossenta, who introduced me to some wonderful examples, and to the long-suffering Gerlinde Reichel, who provided vital English/German translation on the telephone. From the same club I must thank Wolfgang Lichtenfels, too, and also Alois Lenz, who most generously supplied cars to photograph, beer to drink and somewhere to stay! In the Netherlands, I am indebted to Willem & Anna

Derksen, whom I met in Italy, and who have been encouraging ever since! In Amsterdam, Henk Ten Cade (who imports, sells and services Fiat 500s) was generous, both with his time and his cars. I must also thank Charlie Hilm for his willingness to adapt to my own hasty schedule, and Ingrid Knecht who stepped in as a model at the last minute. Thanks also to John Savelkouls, who allowed me to photograph his 850.

The Fiat Club Belgium is enthusiastically presided over by Philippe Bacquaert, who has the rare gift of guiding and encouraging without telling you how to do it; time spent in his company was always a pleasure. Also in Belgium, I must thank Etienne Mertens. Readers familiar with the Family Album VW Beetle and Bus books will know his name in connection with coffee, constantly on the go. He is also an encyclopaedia on all things motoring, and has that kind of energy which makes things happen. So we arrived at the premises of Renaud Beckers one lunchtime, and within the hour had photographed his excellent Abarth.

My biggest surprise of all was the number and quality of Fiats in France. The president of the French club is Jean-Jacques de Galkowsky, himself the author of a book in French on the

Fiat 500, but not at all precious about it, sharing his knowledge of the subject with enthusiasm. (Can anyone ask for more; while politicians wrangle about a united Europe, there are lots of people just getting on with it).

The Gallery section features cars from the Catimini collection of M. Paul Salmon. What started as a day's photography turned into a five-day trip, as I photographed nearly every model in this outstanding collection. M. Salmon also allowed his wacky staff to be used as models, and provided me with the utmost help. Dominique Rival spent days driving me around looking for locations, and then drove little Fiats backwards and forwards while Clothilde Riviere-Prost, Marie-Hélène Langois, Véronique Joncheray and Cécile Stragier lent charm and character to the pictures. Aude Beaupere, M. Salmon's PA, was given the unenviable task of looking after me, co-ordinating cars and models – all the while continuing with her own work – what a star! My thanks to you all.

My thanks also to Victoria Gemmel of Brittany Ferries, who provided me with a superb way of getting to France, via St Malo, on a ship that is almost a floating hotel. This must be by far the nicest way of getting to that part of France - with food as good as any found in a decent French restaurant. The trip, along with the return from Ouistreham, was a pleasure from beginning to end. St Malo was very handy for Nantes, where I photographed the exceptional and rare Weinsberg of Jacques Laubignat.

David Sparrow